Editor
Eric Migliaccio

Cover Artist
Tony Carrillo

Managing Editor
Ina Massler Levin, M.A.

Creative Director
Karen J. Goldfluss, M.S. Ed.

Art Production Manager
Kevin Barnes

Art Coordinator
Renée Christine Yates

Imaging
Leonard P. Swierski

Publisher

Mary D. Smith, M.S. Ed.

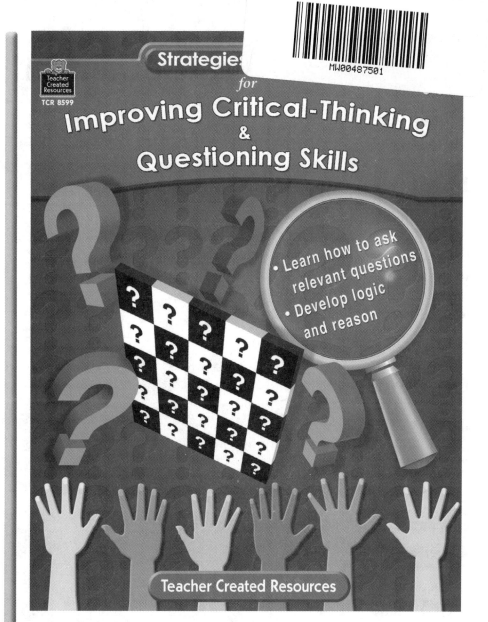

Strategies *for*
Improving Critical-Thinking & Questioning Skills

- Learn how to ask relevant questions
- Develop logic and reason

Teacher Created Resources

Author
Dennis Duncan

Teacher Created Resources, Inc.
6421 Industry Way
Westminster, CA 92683
www.teachercreated.com
ISBN: 978-1-4206-8599-2
© 2007 Teacher Created Resources, Inc.
Made in U.S.A.

Table of Contents

Introduction

Welcome to *Strategies and Games for Improving Critical-Thinking and Questioning* Skills. Much has been written and said about asking questions in the classroom. The focus has been primarily on questions that teachers ask to elicit responses from students. This book takes an entirely different approach. What would happen if a teacher not only allowed but encouraged and taught question-asking by the students? One only has to observe 3- and 4-year-olds as they acquire knowledge; they ask question after question to anyone who will respond. The focus of this book, then, is a series of short "games" that teach students to ask questions to solve the challenge set before them.

The games and strategies presented in this book have been tried and tested in classrooms over the past 20 years. They are designed to teach students thinking strategies and the lively art of asking questions to arrive at solutions to the problems posed for them. The intent is to actively involve the students rather than simply talk to them about problem solving.

Amazing things happen when these games are played. Your students will love the challenge when they sort through the ground rules. Given a simple problem like, "Why are most pencils yellow?" students are asked to solve the problem by asking questions. The tricky part for the teacher is to help the students with the questions without directing them to the answers. Once the students realize they have to solve the problem, they work at it fiercely. In general, students don't like unresolved questions and want to know the solutions.

These games can be played every single day, and most of the games in this book can be repeated over and over again. Each time the game is repeated, there are rules to add to encourage the students to invent new kinds of strategies for solving the problem. For instance, the states games can be used 50 times with a single class, with new rules added each time the game is played—no spelling the state, no using the color, no asking about vowels, etc. The students love the challenge that these changing rules present.

Some fascinating things will take place in your classroom when the games are being played:

- **The students will begin to develop sophisticated thinking strategies and come to view themselves in a more positive light.** Many students who don't memorize well really shine in these exercises. Students who do not write or spell well can become very proficient at asking questions. After time, their overall work will greatly improve as they become more confident in their abilities.

❧ **The students will begin to listen intently to each other and learn from one another.** The teacher's role in this material is to frequently ask the students to explain what they are thinking or how they arrived at a certain idea. Because of that, you will see a lot of students copying another's line of thinking in solving the problem. Because they are often restricted to a certain number of questions as a class, students make sure no questions are wasted.

❧ **Students will learn to expect quiet in the classroom so they can listen.** After a while, you will most likely hear students asking their classmates to quiet down so that everyone can hear the questions asked and the answers given.

The Question Is the Answer

Here is a question: Which teachers have influenced us the most? Most likely, they have been the ones who helped us reach into our own abilities and draw them out. Often, they have done this by challenging us to learn and think autonomously.

There is an old saying: "Give a man a fish, he eats for a day; teach a man how to fish, he eats for a lifetime." Applied to this book, the idea goes like this: Give a student an answer, he learns for a day; teach a student to question, he learns for a lifetime.

Educators know the value of important questions. Most questioning, however, stays on the teacher's side of the desk. Perhaps the grass (of questioning) is greener on the other side of the fence—or greener still with no fence at all.

Question: What if students were coached in the art of asking crucial and imaginative questions and felt validated in doing so?

Question: What if students experienced learning as part of an interactive team, building on the synergy of group exploration?

Answers: Students capable of asking meaningful questions extracted from their own curiosity and awareness can adapt to new and variable challenges. They become capable of significantly higher levels of thinking when they are encouraged to develop questioning skills and when they are allowed to brainstorm with classmates about the questions posed and conclusions derived from information they have received.

Question: Why is effective questioning essential to effective learning?

Answer: In a high-tech world, one may no longer rely on accumulated knowledge and experience but must be able to keep current with creative-thinking/learning skills. Workplaces and schools call for team innovations, strategies, and problem solving.

Questions: What strategies and games work best for teaching students to ask effective questions?

Answer: Keep these five criteria in mind:

- The games should invite consideration of all relevant variables, perspectives, and information.
- The games should apply to student populations that vary by grade level, ability, and curriculum material.
- The games should produce an outcome, resolution, or conclusion.
- Students can be taught the strategies so that they can ask the right types of questions to get the right types of responses.
- The strategies need to be sophisticated enough to account for the complexities of a wide range of issues or dilemmas, yet simple enough so they can be applied by all age and ability levels.

How to Use this Book

Strategies and Games for Improving Critical-Thinking and Questioning Skills contains 18 games, along with teaching notes and game instructions.

Some basic teaching strategies are noted in the beginning pages, and teaching notes are added throughout the book. The teaching notes are sometimes specific to the game on that page and/or can be used as coaching for all games in general. The games do not have to be played in any specific order.

Most games are organized using the following format:

Objective: The same basic objectives apply to all games, with some games having additional and specific objectives.

The Game: What the teacher says/presents to the students to get the game started.

The Rules: What students can and cannot ask in order to make the game interesting and stimulating.

Sample Dialogue: A possible scenario, what the questioning might sound like for that particular game.

Variations:

- For different age groups
- To vary the kinds of skills needed
- To increase the skill level
- To bring out the shy students

Notes: Teaching skills noted, thoughts specific to this particular game, age-specific notes, etc.

About the Games

These exercises are crafted to encourage students to do the following:

1. Ask questions

2. Learn how to process their own thinking.

The games are designed mainly for students in grades 3–5, but these games are versatile and have been used at all levels. They are designed so that obvious answers are just out of reach. At the same time, they are easy enough to stimulate clear and concise questions. The games provide many more ways to teach question-asking than mere guessing games would.

These games enable students to learn more about how they think. One way to think of it is that the player will feel as if he or she is walking down a dark hall in the mind, reading labels on doors until the best one is found. The longer one practices thinking, the easier it becomes to see the labels on the doors. Elegant thinking becomes more natural.

Teachers and administrators may have a few questions of their own:

Question: How can these games be justified when the learning of facts is being neglected?

Answer: These games are offered in the hope that students will feel free to ask questions and will learn on their own. Classroom application of these games has shown this to be the case.

Question: How can this be evaluated and measured?

Answer: If the students are having fun doing these games—and they always do—then consider it useful. Their joy and enthusiasm in learning is the highest evaluation. When students feel free to ask questions, they have what it takes to learn on their own.

Question: If the students are having fun doing these things, can they be useful?

Answer: The fun of these games heightens learning and allows the lessons to sink in much deeper because the students are more open. Never underestimate fun.

The Teacher's Role

Teachers have mastered the questioning process, but students have not. Asking questions and finding answers is an integral part of the education process and the learning process. Ultimately, one of a teacher's main goals is to help students learn to be able to think and reason for themselves.

The teacher's role is critical in making these games effective. First and foremost, the teacher's attitude is to want the students to succeed in solving the problems without giving them the answer. The teacher must learn to listen intently to the students' questions. The teacher must also learn not to lead the students to the correct answer. It is natural and automatic for the students to want instant answers. This is built into our culture. And it is also an automatic reflex for the teacher to want to supply the students with the answers they are tugging and pulling for. Don't give in. Keep the game going—by the rules—for as long as possible. Teachers must be able to teach the students the process of questioning as the game proceeds. The challenge for the teacher is to abstain from leading the students to the answer and instead to let them discover for themselves.

The teacher must stay rooted in the center of the questioning activity, maintaining an internal certainty that the questions are a priority over the answers.

Teacher ingenuity is what makes the games work. Add new rules. Make it exciting.

The Student's Role

- ✌ Students want to be in an atmosphere where questions are allowed.

- ✌ Students need to listen to each other. These games stimulate community spirit.

- ✌ Students will get answers anywhere they can. Once the teacher has engaged the in a question-stimulating game, it is important for the teacher to resist the pull of the students' sense of urgency for answers.

- ✌ Thinking about thinking is very valuable to students and their cognitive processes.

It is amazing how students come up with questions once they feel they are in a non-threatening environment. Teachers can learn a great deal from students by conducting the games. You will probably see groups of students rush to get encyclopedias, dictionaries and atlases during a game. Students have an intense sense of wanting to know.

Team Effort

The games are given to the class to be solved by the class; the entire class tackles them. Team effort is crucial.

Much can be derived from the students' monitoring each other's questions carefully. When students are too focused on their own questions, they often miss key information and do not consider the content of other questions already asked.

Students learn to participate more fully and include those who might normally feel like "outsiders" or be shy when conferencing is encouraged. When the answer is reached, everyone enjoys the success together, not just one or two high achievers. This creates a spirit of community and acceptance amongst the students.

Objectives

All of these games have been played in the classroom, and each has been refined to meet the objectives outlined:

1. To foster cooperation in place of competition.

2. To develop listening/comprehension skills.

3. To provide an atmosphere where question asking is permitted and encouraged.

4. To challenge students as a class to solve a problem by doing the following:
   - asking questions
   - building on each others' questions
   - creating theories to form and test hypotheses, in order to arrive at a final answer

5. To get students to think in images, attributes, and characteristics rather than names of things.

6. To reach a final answer as a group accomplishment, not as just one student's answer.

Information gathered as a result of inquiry tends to stay with students much longer than facts "learned" before the normal forgetting curve takes over.

Teaching Strategies

The goal is to teach skills and techniques that enable the students to get the answers. One important teacher ingredient in these inquiry challenges is to listen carefully to the students' questions. The importance of this cannot be overemphasized. This two-way, teacher/student communication helps create a bond that is strengthened over time.

Answer (Without Giving Away the Answer)

- The students want to solve the problem. The teacher's goal is to get them there without giving them the answer. The teacher's ideal attitude is to want the students to get the answer but to get it on their own.

- Some skill is required on the part of the teacher in answering the questions. The teacher's answers are best if they lead to more questions and maintain the mystery as long as possible without making it too difficult.

- The teacher needs to be sensitive as to when to feed information. (This might be referred to as a teachable moment.) If the students know the teacher will lead them to the correct answer, they become lazy and less creative in their questioning.

- The teacher must be ready to answer many kinds of questions. Sometimes the answer "I don't know" must be used and is acceptable.

Encourage All to Participate

- Employ ways to get the quieter students involved. Insert a rule, for example, that anyone who has asked a question may not ask any of the next five.

- Team up students in groups of four or five. Allow each group to only ask one question. This generally involves most students.

Stimulate Thinking and Participation

- Keep the challenge just in front of them and the atmosphere relaxed.

- When students come up with the "wrong" answer, encourage them to think and ask a new question. Praise them for the thinking they do (if appropriate). After a while, they are quite willing to verbalize their thinking processes, and this helps other students learn thinking and questioning strategies.

- While playing the game, restate the rules or directions whenever necessary.

- Limit students to 10 total questions. Doing this forces them to work together and to monitor each other's questions carefully.

- Stay one step between challenge ("I can get it") and frustration ("It's too hard").

The Mystery Box

Objective: To stimulate questions by means of intense curiosity.

Materials: a sealed box with an object inside

The Game: Students are presented with a box that is taped shut. Say, "I want you to find out what is in the box."

The Rules: Students may hold, shake, lift, or manipulate the box, but they may not look into it. The tricky part is students cannot ask what it is by name (for example, they can't ask "Is it a can opener?"). The following types of questions can be asked:

- What is it made of?
- Is there any writing on it?

- What shape is it?
- What color is it?

Ideally, the students will find out what's in the mystery box through their questioning.

Sample Dialogue
(*S* = student, *T* = teacher)

S: Is it a jackknife?

T: You can't ask that. You could ask, "Is it used to cut things with?"

S: Does it cut things?

T: No.

S: How long is it?

T: Three-and-one-half inches long. Would you like its other dimensions?

T: No.

S: Can you write with it?

T: No—not on paper anyway.

S: Where can I buy it?

T: The local hardware store.

S: What does it cost there?

T: I think one costs about $6.00.

S: Does it have any writing on it?

T: No.

S: Is it made of plastic?

T: No.

The Number Game I

Objective: To teach number concepts

The Game: The teacher makes the statement, "I want you to guess the number I'm thinking of."

Sample Dialogue
(*S* = student, *T* = teacher)

S: 10

T: More.

S: 5

T: More.

S: 12

T: More.

S: 19

T: Less.

(*After the students have played awhile, the teacher adds clues.*)

T: One number is made with curved lines.

T: Both numbers added together make 4.

(*Increase difficulty by introducing fractions.*)

T: I'm thinking of a number between 1 and 5.

S: 3

T: Less.

S: 2

T: More.

Solution: 2 ½.

Variation: Play "Guess My Number, 1–10." In this game, students use no words, they just hold up their fingers. Teacher answers with "more" or "less."

Variation on a Variation: Play "Guess My Number, 1–10" with older students. In this game, students sit with partners, and so they have 20 fingers to work with.

The Number Game II

Objective: Students learn to process numbering.

The Game: The teacher says, "I am thinking of a number. What is it?"

The Rules:

- ❖ Sometimes you may suggest the class can only ask 10 questions.

- ❖ Students are not allowed to ask a direct number question. (For example, "Is it 34?" is not an allowable question.)

Sample Dialogue

(*S* = student, *T* = teacher)

S: Is it more than 100?

T: Yes.

S: Is it even?

T: No, but one of the digits is even.

S: What is the sum of the digits?

T: The sum is an even number less than 10.

S: Are the digits in sequence?

T: No.

S: Is it less than 500?

T: Yes.

S: Is the tens digit greater than the hundreds digit?

T: Yes.

S: Is the hundreds digit even or odd?

3 1 4 2 7 5

The Letter Game

Objective: To develop vocabulary and sound sense.

The Game: The teacher begins by saying, "I want you to guess the letter of the alphabet I'm thinking of."

The Rules: Students may not guess any single letter in a question, such as, "Is it A?" or "Is it B?"

Sample Dialogue
(*S* = student, *T* = teacher)

S: Does this letter start the word *dog*?

T: No.

S: Is it C?

T: You can't ask that—but it is a consonant.

S: Is it made with curved lines?

T: Yes.

S: Does it make the "buh" sound?

T: No, its sound is not made by the lips.

C L Q T Z

Notes: Always the teacher's question to him/herself must be asked, "Should I tell them when the time is up?" You may wait to tell them until next session. This is very effective. The students will continue to think about the game until the next time you meet. They might even discuss the game with their classmates.

The Word Game

Objective: To encourage students to read sentences carefully.

The Game: The teacher presents students with a chart that has a statement, saying, or poem on it. The teacher says, "I am thinking of a word from this poem. You may not say the word." (For examples of appropriate poems to use, see pages 16 and 17.)

Sample Dialogue

(*S* = student, *T* = teacher)

S: Is it on the left side of the paper?

T: No.

S: Is it on the top half?

T: Yes.

S: Does it start with W?

T: It starts with a letter in the first half of the alphabet.

S: How many letters does it have?

T: More than six.

S: Is it a name of a thing?

T: It is not a noun.

Notes: The teacher's task is to give enough information to enable students to keep adding to their stockpile of knowledge until they can come to the answer. As the game is played more times, more rules are added to make the game more challenging.

The Poetry Game

Objectives:

➥ To get the students to carefully read a poem.

➥ To learn some of the poems' meanings.

➥ To experience reading poetry aloud.

Materials: copies or overhead transparencies of several poems (Begin with shorter poems (see page 16 for haikus) and advance to longer poems (see page 17).)

The Game: Students are presented with a poem in large lettering. The teacher says, "I am thinking of a word in the poem. What is it?"

The Rules: Students may not ask single-word questions. You may wish to add rules in subsequent games (no using parts of speech, no using number of syllables, etc.).

Sample Dialogue
(*S* = student, *T* = teacher)

S: Is it a noun?

T: What is your definition of a noun?

S: A noun is a person, place, or thing.

T: It is not a noun.

S: Is it in the top half of the poem?

T: (*dividing the poem in half*) No, it is not.

S: How many syllables does the word have?

T: It has more than two.

S: What letter does the word start with?

T: The word starts with a letter in the first half of the alphabet.

The Poetry Game *(cont.)*

Haikus

A Giant Firefly

A giant firefly:
that way, this way, that way, this—
and it passes by.

~Kobayashi Issa

After Killing a Spider

After killing
a spider, how lonely I feel
in the cold of night!

~Masaoka Shiki

That Wren

That wren—
looking here, looking there.
You lose something?

~Kobayashi Issa

An Old Pond

An old pond;
A frog jumps in—
The sound of water.

~Matsuo Basho

The Poetry Game (cont.)

Poems

Fog

The fog comes   over harbor and city
on little cat feet.   on silent haunches,
It sits looking   and then moves on.

~Carl Sandburg

Good Hours

I had for my winter evening walk—
No one at all with whom to talk,
But I had the cottages in a row
Up to their shining eyes in snow.
And I thought I had the folk within:
I had the sound of a violin;
I had a glimpse through curtain laces
Of youthful forms and youthful faces.
I had such company outward bound.
I went till there were no cottages found.
I turned and repented, but coming back
I saw no window but that was black.
Over the snow my creaking feet
Disturbed the slumbering village street
Like profanation, by your leave,
At ten o'clock of a winter eve.

~Robert Frost

The Multiplication Grid Game

Objectives:

- To help students learn multiplication facts.
- To promote the use of reasoning skills.

The Game: Students are presented with a chart of the multiplication tables. Say to the students, "I'm thinking of a number on the chart. What number am I thinking of?"

Materials: copies or an overhead transparency of the game grid on page 19

The Rules: You may not use a single- or double-digit guess (such as "Is it 3?" or "Is it 45?").

Sample Dialogue

(*S* = student, *T* = teacher)

S: Is it even?

T: No.

S: If I divided the chart into four sections, what part would it be in?

T: Bottom right.

S: If I added the two numbers together, would the answer be 9?

T: No, but the answer would be an odd number.

	0x	1x	2x	3x	4x	5x	6x	7x	8x	9x
0x	0	0	0	0	0	0	0	0	0	0
1x	0	1	2	3	4	5	6	7	8	9
2x	0	2	4	6	8	10	12	14	16	18
3x	0	3	6	9	12	15	18	21	24	27
4x	0	4	8	12	16	20	24	28	32	36
5x	0	5	10	15	20	25	30	35	40	45
6x	0	6	12	18	24	30	36	42	48	54
7x	0	7	14	21	28	35	42	49	56	63
8x	0	8	16	24	32	40	48	56	64	72
9x	0	9	18	27	36	45	54	63	72	81

The Game Grid

	0x	1x	2x	3x	4x	5x	6x	7x	8x	9x
0x	0	0	0	0	0	0	0	0	0	0
1x	0	1	2	3	4	5	6	7	8	9
2x	0	2	4	6	8	10	12	14	16	18
3x	0	3	6	9	12	15	18	21	24	27
4x	0	4	8	12	16	20	24	28	32	36
5x	0	5	10	15	20	25	30	35	40	45
6x	0	6	12	18	24	30	36	42	48	54
7x	0	7	14	21	28	35	42	49	56	63
8x	0	8	16	24	32	40	48	56	64	72
9x	0	9	18	27	36	45	54	63	72	81

The Grandma Game

Objective: To stimulate investigation beyond the obvious.

The Game: The teacher presents the class with a problem and asks the students to find the common solution.

The Rules:

1. To play this game, you must tell me what Grandma likes first and what she doesn't like second.

2. Listen carefully to the clues. You might have to do some guessing at first.

3. If you can do three in a row correctly, you probably have the answer.

Sample Dialogue

(*S* = student, *T* = teacher)

T: Grandma likes pepper but not salt. Grandma likes puppies, not dogs. Grandma likes cheese and not milk.

S: Grandma likes pigs but not piglets.

T: Grandma doesn't like either.

S: Grandma likes paper but not ink.

T: Grandma doesn't like either one.

S: Grandma likes kittens but not cats.

T: You are correct. Give me another example that has not been said.

S: I pass.

S: Grandma likes chicken but not beef.

T: Grandma likes beef but not chicken.

• •

Solution: Grandma likes things that have double letters in them; she doesn't like things that don't.

Notes: Try writing the "like" list and the "not like" list on the board.

Variations: The wonderful part of the game is that the rules can be changed.

•❥ Grandma likes cheese but not eggs. She likes salt but not tortillas.
  (*The last letter of the first word is the same the first letter of the second word.*)

•❥ Grandma likes pears but not pumpkins. She likes boys but not children.
  (*She likes words with one syllable, not words with more than one.*)

? ?

The Dictionary Game

Objective:

- To help students eliminate large chunks of information that is irrelevant to the answer. This is a constant problem in these games, and this game helps resolve that issue.

Materials: one dictionary per every 2 to 4 students

The Game: Say to the class, "I want you to find the word I am thinking of."

The Rules: You have 15 guesses as a class. The end of the game comes when a group agrees on the word by simply pointing to it.

Sample Dialogue

(*S* = student, *T* = teacher)

S: Is the word in the first half of the dictionary?

T: The word begins with a letter that is in the first half of the alphabet.

S: Is it dog?

T: No. Remember, we have 15 questions only. Do you think that was a good question? Do you want to take it back?

S: How many letters does it have?

T: Six.

S: What letter does it start with?

T: B.

S: How many vowels does it have?

T: Two. Now, turn to the start of the B section and find the end of the B section. How could you ask questions that would eliminate the Bs that aren't it?

S: I don't get it.

T: Well, you could ask about the second letter. You could ask if it is a vowel.

S: Is the second letter a vowel?

T: Yes, it is a U.

Variation: Hand out thesauruses and play "The Thesaurus Game."

The States Game

Objective:

- To encourage thinking "outside the box."

Materials: a map of the United States (see page 23)

The Game: The teacher says, "I am thinking of a state. I want you to ask questions and guess which state it is."

The Rules: You may not say the name of the state during the entire game.

Sample Dialogue

(*S* = student, *T* = teacher)

S: Is it a big state?

T: What do you mean by "big"?

S: Is it one of the five largest states by area?

T: No, it is not.

S: How many syllables are there in its name?

T: One.

S: What letter of the alphabet does it start with?

T: A letter in the first half of the alphabet.

Variations: It is very productive to play this game over and over with the same class. With each successive game, a new rule or prohibition is added. You might wish to start the next game with no state-names questions. If the game is presented as a friendly challenge, students really respond with many new ideas and questions. If they aren't allowed to use beginning letters, they use last letters or descriptions of the state's shape. Another variation is to use "if" questions:

- "If I draw a line through the states on the perimeter of the map, would it touch your state?"

- "If I divided the map into four sections, in which section would this state be?"

The States Game (cont.)

Map of the United States

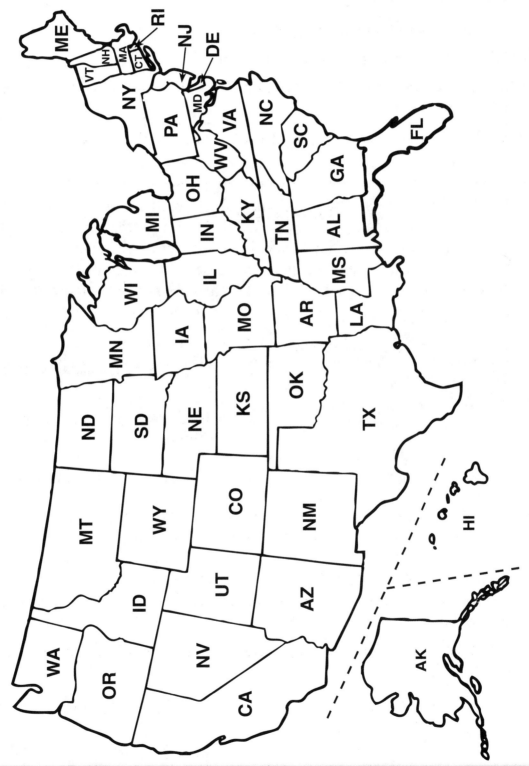

The Analogies Game

Objectives:

- ➤ To explore analogies.
- ➤ To explore the data-theory cycle.
- ➤ To teach a process.

The Game: The teacher writes a simple analogy on the board and explains it briefly.

> *A : Z :: B : ?*   *A is to Z as B is to what?*

Students should learn to analyze the relationship between the two letters in the first part of the analogy. In this case, the letters A and Z stand for themselves. What is the relationship between these two letters? A is the first letter of alphabet, and Z is the last. Then students should look at the letter given in the second part of the analogy, B. They then need to ask themselves, "What letter would have the same relationship to B that A has to Z?" The answer is Y. (B is the second letter of the alphabet, and Y is the second to last letter of the alphabet.)

Some students will get the relationship right away. The objective is to have a discussion of relationships. Use other simple analogies (e.g., 2 : 3 :: 5 : ?) until students have a grasp of them. In cases where letters represent words, you may wish to provide students with all four parts of the analogy.

Then write the game analogy and proceed with the class asking questions. Analogies are almost always solved in about 15 minutes. The artistry of each session is to know how much information to give to the students.

This is a great introduction to the study of analogies and the pertinent thinking process. The answer is just out of reach, and with encouragement for getting into the process, students respond well.

Eventually, some student will come up with the correct answer. It usually is a loud "Aha!" Discuss that moment with the class. Ask, "What happens when the right answer comes? What happens inside you?" It is a good springboard for discussions about the thinking process. The thrill that comes from the discovery of the answer is worth all the grumbling of students beginning the process. The teacher must want the students to succeed and must be willing to withhold the answer. The point of the game is to reach a process. The answer is of secondary importance.

The Analogies Game (cont.)

Here are several examples of analogies from different curriculum areas:

From Social Studies

➥ P : F :: R : I (*Paris* is to *France* as *Rome* is to *Italy*.)

From Mathematics

➥ S : 4 :: O : 8 (*Square* is to *4* [sides] as *octagon* is to *8*.)

From Language Arts

➥ P : D :: Q : I (*Period* is to *declarative* as *question mark* is to *interrogative*.)

From Science

➥ S : R :: H : M (*Snake* is to *reptile* as *human* is to *mammal*.)

Here is a sample dialogue of the discussion that could take place while students try to solve the following analogy: S : D :: W : O (The answer is "sand is to desert as water is to ocean.")

Sample Dialogue

(*S* = student, *T* = teacher)

T: Your job is to ask questions to solve this analogy puzzle: S : D :: W : O

S: Do these letters stand for words?

T: Yes, and they are all nouns.

S: What do they stand for?

T: The object of what we are doing is for you to ask the right questions. I'm not here to tell you the answers.

S: This is too hard.

T: It is hard, but I know that you can solve it. Don't give up so easily.

S: How many vowels does the D word have?

T: Two. Both vowels are E.

Card Games

Objectives:

- ❖ To learn patience.

- ❖ To focus on the process of elimination with each question. Because the cards are tangible and they can be eliminated with each question, students experience the value of using each answer to eliminate possibilities and thereby narrow them.

Materials: one deck of cards per student (Make sure students count their own deck and do not share cards with each other.)

The Game: "I am thinking of a card in your deck. When this game is finished, you are to be holding just the card I am thinking of."

Sample Dialogue

(*S* = student, *T* = teacher)

S: Is it red?

T: No. Discard what it isn't. *(Give students time to discard all red cards.)*

S: Is it a palace-people card?

T: No. *(Give students time to discard all black palace people cards.)*

S: Is it a 7?

T: No. *(Remind students of strategies that eliminate a large number of cards.)*

S: Is it even?

T: No. *(Give students time to discard all even-numbered cards.)*

Notes: The game continues until the correct card is left in the student's hand. If they want to guess before the last card, they should hold up the card they think it is. This is considered a question.

Variations:

1. Give students only 10 or fewer guesses as a class.

2. Have students work in teams of two or teams of four.

The Month Game

Objective:

- To stretch the students' thinking abilities.

The Game: The teacher poses the question, "I am thinking of a month in the year." As a class, the entire group has five questions to guess what it is. You may use any strategy only one time. Questions like "Is it December?" are not good strategy.

Sample Dialogue

(*S* = student, *T* = teacher)

S: Is it in the first half of the year?

T: Yes.

S: How many days does it have in it?

T: It has more than 30.

S: Does it have a holiday in it?

T: Yes, but most months do. You have three more guesses. Let's take time now to conference. You may talk to anyone in the room but me. Share ideas and strategies.

(The conferences are productive, but keep the conference time less than a minute.)

Variations:

- Let five students take a stab at it, with each student getting one question each.

- Give the class 10 questions, but they may never say the name of a month.

Notes: The point of the game is to keep the answer out in front of the students and have fun. Students enjoy the challenge if it is kept light and if the reason for doing this is constantly explained.

The Grid Game

Objective:

❧ To let students discover patterns.

The Game: Introduce students to the game by drawing a grid on the board and labelling it as shown here:

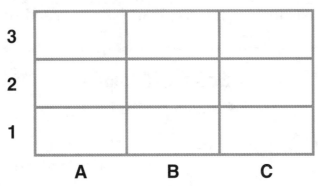

The students are shown grids that contain nine boxes. Only one or a few of the boxes are filled in. The students have to figure out how to fill in the rest of the boxes. Pick an easy game to begin with and progress to more difficult games. There are many sample games provided on page 29–31.

The Rules: The teacher says, "I want you to figure out the numbers that appear in these boxes. I have a number pattern that I want you to discover. Raise your hand, say a number, and tell me where it fits." Often the first guesses have to be just guesses, but there are some questions that make the process easier. For example, you might ask:

❧ What is the range of numbers?

❧ Is the pattern horizontal, vertical, diagonal or random?

❧ Are all of the spaces filled up?

The teacher can just let students struggle at the beginning, but often the teacher will need to explain the meanings of horizontal, vertical, diagonal, or random.

Notes: This game and its variations are almost endless. Students love the challenge and get quite skilled at asking more and more sophisticated questions. Your own creativity can expand the game in many directions. Consider limiting students to 10 questions per class. Doing this forces them to work together and to monitor each other's questions carefully.

Sample Game

	A	B	C
3			
2		15	
1			

Sample Dialogue
(*S* = student, *T* = teacher)

S: Is there a 14 at A2?

T: There is no 14 in this puzzle.

S: Are there any even numbers?

T: Yes.

S: Please put a 20 at B3.

T: A 20 does not fit there. Tell me what you are thinking.

S: I am counting by fives going across.

T: That's great thinking, but that is not for this one. Try counting by another number.

S: Put a 12 in A2.

T: Tell me what you are thinking.

S: I am counting by three going across.

T: A 12 in A2 is correct.

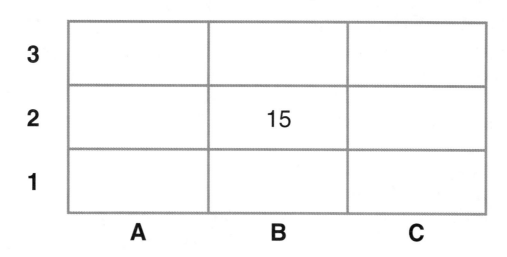

	A	B	C
3	3	6	9
2	12	15	18
1	21	24	27

The Grid Game (cont.)

More Sample Games

3	1	3	6
2	2	5	8
1	4	7	9
	A	**B**	**C**

Solution: numbers in order (diagonally)

3	W	A	J
2	M	M	A
1	J	VB	H
	A	**B**	**C**

Solution: first nine U.S. presidents (horizontally)

3	T	H	E
2	R	E	D
1	C	A	R
	A	**B**	**C**

Solution: a simple phrase (horizontally)

3	P	N	D
2	Q	HD	D
1	F	T	T
	A	**B**	**C**

Solution: American currency—starting with the penny (horizontally)

3	J	A	J
2	F	M	A
1	M	J	S
	A	**B**	**C**

Solution: months of the year (vertically)

3	YELLOW	GREEN	GRASS
2	CHEESE	PEPPER	THREE
1	SPELL	GALLON	BEETS
	A	**B**	**C**

Solution: words with double letters (random)

More Sample Games (cont.)

3	M	E	S
2	V	J	N
1	M	U	P
	A	**B**	**C**

Solution: planets—in order from the sun (diagonally)

3	1	1	2
2	3	5	8
1	13	21	34
	A	**B**	**C**

Solution: add the previous number (horizontally)

3	TUBA	LAND	LOG
2	CLUB	EDGE	HIGH
1	TALC	STAFF	HAWAII
	A	**B**	**C**

Solution: alphabetical order by last letter (vertically)

3	17	62	143
2	44	611	80
1	71	152	1,313
	A	**B**	**C**

Solution: sum of digits equal eight (random)

3	8	5	4
2	9	1	7
1	6	3	2
	A	**B**	**C**

Solution: numbers in alphabetical order (horizontally)

3	C	CF	1B
2	LF	P	RF
1	2B	SS	3B
	A	**B**	**C**

Solution: baseball positions in alphabetical order (horizontally)

The Equations Game

Objective:

❧ To present a different kind of problem, one that is often solved with an "Aha!" or getting the whole thing at once.

The Game: Teacher presents the class with an equation—one in which letters stand for words. Students are asked to solve it. The teacher should familiarize the students with the equations by giving the following example:

> $3F = 1Y$ *Solution: 3 FEET equals 1 YARD.*

The Rules: Write this equation on the board: $N + P + SM = the\ S\ of\ C$. Then say, "I want you to solve this equation by asking questions."

Sample Dialogue
(*S* = student, *T* = teacher)

S: Do these letters stand for words?

T: Yes.

S: What are the vowels?

T: If I told you one of the words you would know the whole puzzle.

S: Can you give us a clue, a place to start?

T: They are nouns.

S: Are these nouns something you could see?

T: They could have been seen a long time ago, but not now.

S: Do they have something to do with history?

T: Yes.

S: Is it something we study in school?

T: Yes, in social studies class.

• •

Solution: NINA + PINTA + SANTA MARIA = the SHIPS of COLUMBUS

Notes: See pages 33 and 34 for more examples of equations that work well for this game.

? ?

The Equations Game (cont.)

Sample Equations

The following word equations have been used in the classroom. They can be difficult—but not impossible—for grade-school students.

#	Equation	Solution
1.	4 = S on a S	4 = SIDES on a SQUARE
2.	a B in the H = 2 in the B	a BIRD in the HAND = TWO in the BUSH
3.	8D – 24H = 1W	8 DAYS minus 24 HOURS = 1 WEEK
4.	1Y + 24H = 1LY	1 YEAR + 24 HOURS = 1 LEAP YEAR
5.	3 = W on a T	3 = WHEELS on a TRICYCLE
6.	6 = L on an I	6 = LEGS on an INSECT
7.	7 = C in the W	7 = CONTINENTS in the WORLD
8.	E – 8 = Z	EIGHT minus 8 equals ZERO
9.	R = C of a SS	RED = COLOR of a STOP SIGN
10.	1 + 6Z = 1M	1 + 6 ZEROES = 1 MILLION

Sample Equations *(cont.)*

#	Equation	Solution
11.	23Y – 3Y =2D	23 YEARS minus 3 YEARS = 2 DECADES
12.	19D + 20N = 20D	19 DOLLARS + 20 NICKELS = 20 DOLLARS
13.	3D = 18P	3 DOZEN = 18 PAIRS
14.	18 = H on a GC	18 = HOLES on a GOLF COURSE
15.	S + M + T + W + T + S + S = DOTW	SUN. + MON. + TUES. + WED. + THURS. + FRI. + SAT. = DAYS OF THE WEEK
16.	R + O + Y + G + B + I + V = C of a R	RED + ORANGE + YELLOW + GREEN + BLUE + INDIGO + VIOLET = COLORS of a RAINBOW
17.	M + V + E + M + J + S + U + N + P = P of the SS	MERCURY + VENUS + EARTH + MARS + JUPITER + SATURN + URANUS + NEPTUNE + PLUTO = PLANETS of the SOLAR SYSTEM
18.	M + M + NH + V + C + RI = the NES	MAINE + MASSACHUSETTS + NEW HAMPSHIRE + VERMONT + CONNECTICUT + RHODE ISLAND = the NEW ENGLAND STATES

Soma Cubes

Soma cubes are a great way to build critical-thinking skills, and students respond to the challenge that they bring. Working with the cubes will not be like many of the other strict question-and-answer problem-solving sessions presented in this book, but this activity does encourage the same type of thinking skills.

These cubes are available for purchase online. If you prefer, you can use the cube template on page 36 to make sets of cubes for your classroom. This does require some time and energy, but it will be well spent.

The cubes come in the seven individual pieces shown here. Each student will need a set of these seven pieces.

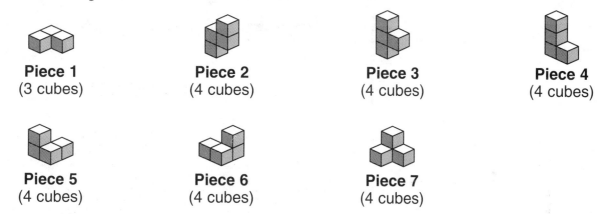

Piece 1
(3 cubes)

Piece 2
(4 cubes)

Piece 3
(4 cubes)

Piece 4
(4 cubes)

Piece 5
(4 cubes)

Piece 6
(4 cubes)

Piece 7
(4 cubes)

It takes 27 cubes to make a complete set of these seven pieces. The students are presented with the cubes and asked to make a large cube with them. (There are many correct ways to do this.) Students can ask questions as they go.

Objective:

    ➤ To create a hands-on, three-dimensional experience in problem solving.

The Game: Say, "I want you to be sure you have all seven pieces to start with. Assemble the seven pieces to make a cube." If needed, draw a cube on the board or have a visual prop to show them what you expect them to make.

Walk around and ask students questions about how they are attacking the problem of making a cube. Having played several of the games in this book at this point, students will have become familiar with the process of asking questions. Encourage them to work together but not to share pieces.

Some students solve the problem quickly. Have them do it again or have them help others. Set up a rule where those who finish early are not permitted to handle another student's blocks but can help by using words.

The next time you play this game, have students try to complete Shape 1 from page 37. Ask them to visualize the pieces and then try to put them together just thinking about it. Both page 37 and 38 contain several shapes to challenge students. These are just suggestions. Choose any shape on any given day.

Cube Template

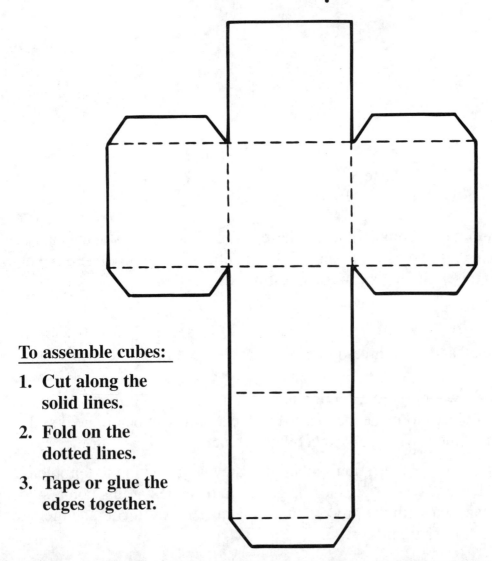

To assemble cubes:

1. Cut along the solid lines.

2. Fold on the dotted lines.

3. Tape or glue the edges together.

Shapes to Build

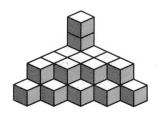

Shape 1

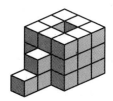

Shape 2

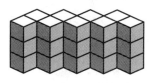

Shape 3

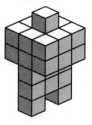

Shape 4

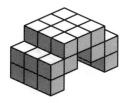

Shape 5

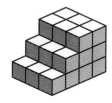

Shape 6

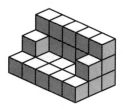

Shape 7

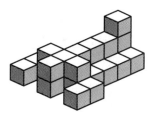

Shape 8

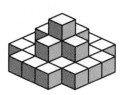

Shape 9

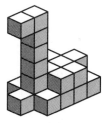

Shape 10

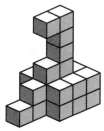

Shape 11

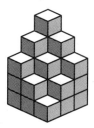

Shape 12

More Shapes to Build

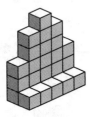

Shape 13

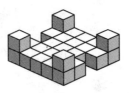

Shape 14

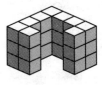

Shape 15

Shape 16

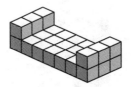

Shape 17

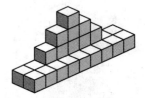

Shape 18

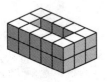

Shape 19

Shape 20

Shape 21

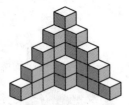

Shape 22

Shape 23

Shape 24

The Shapes Chart Game

Objective:

- ➡ To develop concentration skills.

Tools: the shapes charts on pages 40 and 41

The Game: The teacher presents the chart and says, "I am thinking of a shape on this chart. Guess what it is. Use your questioning skills to find out."

Sample Dialogue

(*S* = student, *T* = teacher)

S: Is it in the top row?

T: No, but it is on the perimeter of the chart.

S: What does *perimeter* mean?

T: It means "the outside or edge."

Variation: Allow the students to ask two question at one time.

The Game: The teacher presents the chart and says, "I am thinking of a shape on the chart. I want you to guess what it is. The questioning is different now; I want you to ask two questions at a time, like 'Is it gray and on the perimeter?' I will answer your questions in one of three ways:

1. 'One of those is true.'   3. 'Both are true.'

2. 'Neither of those is true.'

I will not tell you which one is true if I answer, 'One is true.' How do you think you will know if a question is true or not?" Allow the class to discuss this, but do not give too much explanation yet.

Sample Dialogue

(*S* = student, *T* = teacher)

T: I have a figure on the chart. Guess what it is by asking double questions.

S: Is it gray and small?

T: Neither of those is true.

S: Is it white and small?

T: One of those is true.

S: Which one?

T: I can't tell you, but let's work together to find out. Does the group have a strategy to help solve this problem?

? ?

The Shapes Chart Game (cont.)

After the game has been played for a while with some hits and misses, the students catch on to strategies. It is best to let them flounder some rather than give too much explanation. They listen better after the problem is firmly fixed in their mind.

Variation: Sometimes prohibit the saying of a shape or color or size to provide more challenge. Only do this after students have played the game several times.

Notes: Teachers are encouraged to use whatever strategies necessary to get all of the students to participate in the question-asking (no one who has asked a question so far is eligible to ask, only one question is allowed per group, the next question can only come from this half of the room, etc.).

Shapes Chart I

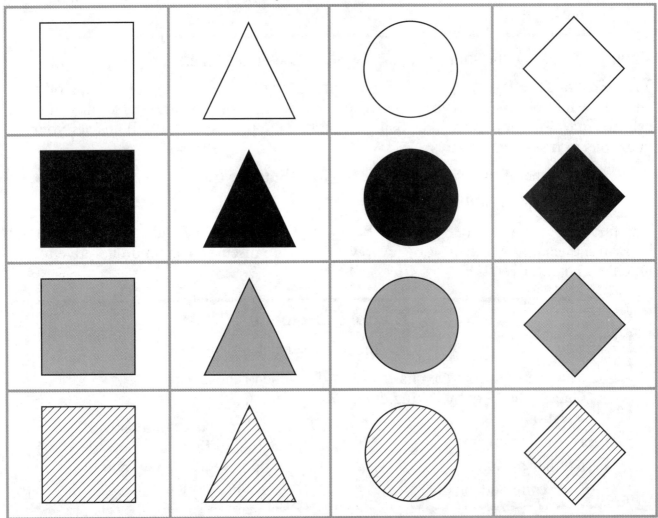

Shapes Chart II

Which One Doesn't Belong?

Objectives:

- To learn how to ask specific questions.
- To test ideas/theories.

The Game: Say, "I am going to write six words on the chalkboard. One of them does not belong." Write these words on the chalkboard:

> *stare*   *effort*   *about*   *notice*   *show*   *absolute*

Materials: the game cards on pages 43 and 44, the answer key on page 45

Sample Dialogue

(*S* = student, *T* = teacher)

T: Which of these words doesn't belong with the rest?

S: *Stare.*

T: Why did you pick that one?

S: Is it the only one without an *o*.

T: Good thinking. That is not the answer I had in mind, but you've given a great answer. For my answer, I could write *store*, and the correct answer would not change.

S: If I changed the order of the words, would it make a difference?

T: Are you asking if you should put the words in alphabetical order? No, that is good thinking, though. That was a great "if" question. "If" questions are powerful tools that are often used in experiments.

S: Does it have anything to do with the meaning of the words?

T: No, but that is useful information. We don't have to look there anymore for answers.

S: Does it have anything to do with letters in the words?

T: Yes, it does.

Notes: This game is engaging and challenging to students. The possibilities are endless. This game is useful for small chunks of time because the session for each one is short.

Which One Doesn't Belong?

Game Cards

1.		2.		3.	
pizza	apples	artichoke	alligator	potatoes	yams
pears	cheese	crocodile	aardvark	tomatoes	turnips
balloons	green	armadillo	apple	beets	carrots

4.		5.		6.	
celery	salary	A	F	Washington	California
beets	berries	T	V	Goergia	Illinois
cheese	elephants	W	B	Ohio	Canada

7.		8.		9.	
gate	Ohio	Louisiana	Colorado	Mercury	Moon
Indiana	chili	Missouri	Illinois	Saturn	Neptune
Wisconsin	Seattle	Minnesota	Arkansas	Saturn	Earth

10.		11.		12.	
Washington	Minnesota	Washington	Ohio	one	forty-four
New York	Idaho	Canada	advance	seventeen	three
Iowa	Montana	speedily	New York	twenty-nine	eleven

Game Cards (cont.)

13.		14.		15.	
161	noon	2	3	Alabama	Georgia
pop	2112	19	22	Washington	Colorado
4343	level	37	43	Kansas	Iowa

16.		17.		18.	
Washington	Jefferson	January	March	Los Angeles	Salem
Lincoln	Franklin	August	July	Boise	Springfield
Fillmore	Garfield	October	September	Jackson	Boston

19.		20.		21.	
300	93	LE	LS	hydrogen	oxygen
27	60	LO	LW	silver	gold
444	14	LH	LM	aluminum	salt

22.		23.		24.	
soccer	volleyball	red	green	246	314
tennis	golf	yellow	blue	268	422
ice hockey	baseball	white	gold	224	156

Which One Doesn't Belong (cont.)

Answer Key

Display this list on an overhead projector or have copies available. Encourage students to devise some puzzles their own use. It is valuable practice for students to be in the teacher role of answering the questions.

1. **Doesn't Belong:** pears (the other words contain double letters)
2. **Doesn't Belong:** crocodile (the other words begin with A)
3. **Doesn't Belong:** tomatoes (the other words have two E's in them)
5. **Doesn't Belong:** B (the others are made only with straight lines)
6. **Doesn't Belong:** Goergia (the others are spelled correctly)
7. **Doesn't Belong:** Wisconsin (the others end with in vowels)
8. **Doesn't Belong:** Colorado (the other states border the Mississippi River)
9. **Doesn't Belong:** Moon (the others are planets)
10. **Doesn't Belong:** Iowa (the other states border Canada)
11. **Doesn't Belong:** New York (the others each have three vowels)
12. **Doesn't Belong:** forty-four (the other numbers are odd numbers)
13. **Doesn't Belong:** 4343 (the others are palindromes—the same backwards or forwards)
14. **Doesn't Belong:** 22 (the other numbers are prime numbers)
15. **Doesn't Belong:** Washington (the first letters of the other states are from the first half of alphabet)
16. **Doesn't Belong:** Franklin (the others were U.S. presidents)
17. **Doesn't Belong:** September (the other months have 31 days)
18. **Doesn't Belong:** Los Angeles (the other cities are state capitals)
19. **Doesn't Belong:** 14 (the other numbers are divisible by 3)
20. **Doesn't Belong:** LW (the others are the initials of the Great Lakes)
21. **Doesn't Belong:** salt (the others are elements)
22. **Doesn't Belong:** ice hockey (the other sports use a ball)
23. **Doesn't Belong:** yellow (the other colors contain only one syllable)
24. **Doesn't Belong:** 422 (in the other numbers, the third digit is the sum of the first two digits)

The Decimal Game

Objectives:

- ◦• To explore decimal names.

- ◦• To use reasoning skills.

- ◦• To learn how to be precise in questioning.

- ◦• To learn to listen to others.

Materials: a chart of decimals (see page 47)

The Game: The teacher will pick out a decimal from the chart; the students will figure out which one it is by asking questions. (The teacher may wish to review tenths, hundredths, thousandths, ones, tens, etc., with the class before beginning this game.)

The Rules: There is only one rule: If the strategy has been used once, it may not be used again.

Sample Dialogue

(*S* = student, *T* = teacher)

S: Is it in column one?

T: No, it is in an even-numbered column.

S: Is it in column four?

T: That strategy has been used already.

S: How many digits did it have?

T: Five.

S: What row is it in?

T: It is in a vowel row.

S: What is the sum of the digits?

T: Fourteen.

S: Where is the dot (decimal point)?

T: It has no place greater than ones (review ones, tens, etc.).

• •

Solution: 3.1415, which is located at 4I on the chart.

The Decimal Game (cont.)

Decimals Chart

	1	2	3	4	5	6	7
A	1.1	21.5	1.07	1.4	.008	9.99	.8
B	.1	.007	.0007	8.88	.006	1.06	.92
C	1.01	5.51	1.8	.001	6.009	1.3	.7
D	1.004	.2	.005	1.05	86	123.1	0.09
E	.3	11.11	1.2	.123	12.344	.6	1.0
F	1.04	.004	21.05	1.02	1.002	1.03	.1
G	4	5.51	1.09	.4	60.66	11.11	.111
H	1.6	.003	22	4.44	.5	1.5	67.89
I	9.011	1.06	1.7	3.1415	.002	.102	.000

The Calendar Game

Objectives:

- To apply math skills.
- To learn questioning strategies.
- To solve problems as a class.
- To learn to listen to others.

Materials: a few calendars (can be from any year); to begin with, use one of the sample calendar pages provided on page 49

The Game: The teacher presents a page of a yearly calendar. The students must find a specific day, month, and year—without directly asking what month, day, or year it is. The students must use precise questioning to find out about the calendar. They should talk quietly to their neighbor before beginning to develop some strategies (conference). Allowing about one minute works best.

Sample Dialogue

(*S* = student, *T* = teacher)

S: Is the number even or odd?

T: Even.

S: What is the sum of the digits?

T: If you add the diagonals any place on the calendar, the sums are equal. I'll call these cross sums. The cross sum is 26.

S: Is the number rounded or straight?

T: It is rounded.

S: What column is it in?

T: The sum of the digits in the column is 75.

S: This is hard!

T: Yes, it is hard, but I think you can do it.

S: Is the day a school day?

T: Yes.

S: Is it the last day of the week?

The Calendar Game (cont.)

Sample Calendars

January

Sunday	Monday	Tuesday	Wednesday	Thursday	Friday	Saturday
	1	2	3	4	5	6
7	8	9	10	11	12	13
14	15	16	17	18	19	20
21	22	23	24	25	26	27
28	29	30	31			

September

Sunday	Monday	Tuesday	Wednesday	Thursday	Friday	Saturday
						1
2	3	4	5	6	7	8
9	10	11	12	13	14	15
16	17	18	19	20	21	22
23	24	25	26	27	28	29
30						

The Month Game

Objectives:

- To review months of the year.
- To develop precise questioning strategies.
- To develop new and innovative ideas.

The Game: The teacher thinks of a month of the year. The students try to guess it in seven guesses, but they may not say the name of a month in their question.

Sample Dialogue

(*S* = student, *T* = teacher)

S: Is it January?

T: You can't say that because of our rules. Remember you only get seven guesses. Do you want an answer, or do you want to withdraw the question?

S: I withdraw the question.

T: You have seven guesses left. Make your questions good ones.

S: Do we go to school during this month?

T: Yes.

S: What letter does the month begin with?

T: It begins with a letter in the second half of the alphabet.

S: How many letters does it have?

T: Let me think about that. Okay, the month has an odd number of letters. You have four questions left.

Note: This is a great, 10-minute game that will fill in short blocks of time throughout the day.

Variation: Play the Year Game. Think of a year and encourage students to ask questions to figure out the answer. Give them clues, such as the following:

- events that happened in that year
- the odd or even status of the digits in the year
- the sum of the digits in the year

The Flag Game

Objectives:

- Sort objectives by attributes.
- Develop questioning strategies.
- Learn to listen to other questions for clues

Materials: examples of country flags (see pages 52–53); for best results, copy, color, laminate, and cut out the flags provided

The Game: The teacher says, "I am thinking of a certain country's flag. Which one is it?" The students must carefully assess the chart and ask questions. Students may not directly ask which country the flag is from.

Sample Dialogue

(*S* = student, *T* = teacher)

S: Does it have any green in it?

T: No.

S: Does it have a design on it?

T: I will tell you this: it is not symmetrical.

S: What does that mean?

T: If you divided the flag in half from left to right, both halves would not look the same.

S: Does the country's name start with a vowel?

T: No. It starts with a consonant in the first half of the alphabet.

S: Is the country in Europe?

T: Yes, it is.

The Flag Game (cont.)

Country Flags

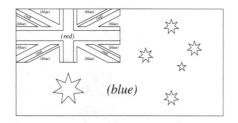

Australia

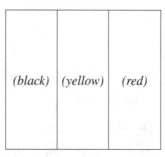

Belgium

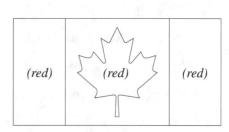

Canada

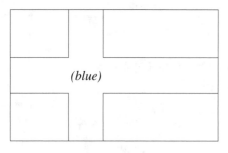

Finland

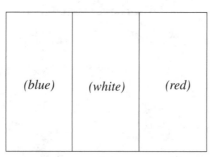

France

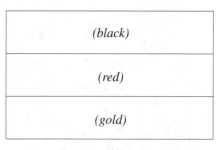

Germany

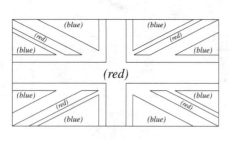

Great Britain

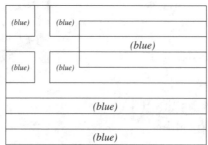

Greece

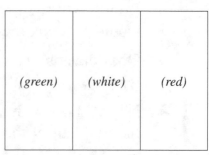

Italy

The Flag Game (cont.)

More Country Flags

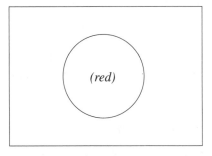

Japan

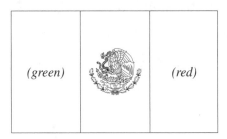

Mexico

Netherlands

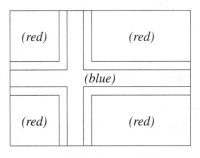

Norway

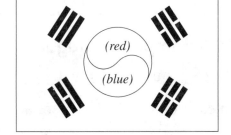

South Korea

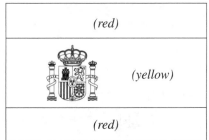

Spain

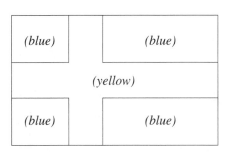

Sweden

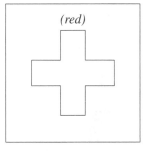

Switzerland

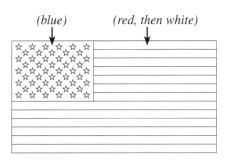

United States

The Tile Game

Objectives:

- To have students work in groups effectively.
- To develop questioning skills.
- To develop spatial relationships through visualization.
- To listen carefully.

Materials: ceramic tiles (about 25 per group); if ceramic tiles aren't available, cut out and laminate several copies of the tiles from page 55

The Game: The teacher thinks of a shape. The students must ask questions and move their tiles into that shape, then raise their hands when they are done. They must listen carefully to the teacher's answers because the shape they make must be agreed upon by everyone. The students must ask five questions before they shape their tiles.

Sample Dialogue

(*S* = student, *T* = teacher)

S: Do all the tiles touch each other?

T: No.

S: Do I use all the tiles?

T: No, but you use an odd number of them.

S: Is the odd number greater than 10?

T: There are 13 tiles.

S: Are they all in a row?

T: No.

S: Do they all form a shape?

T: Yes.

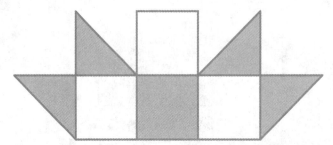

The Tile Game (cont.)

Game Tiles

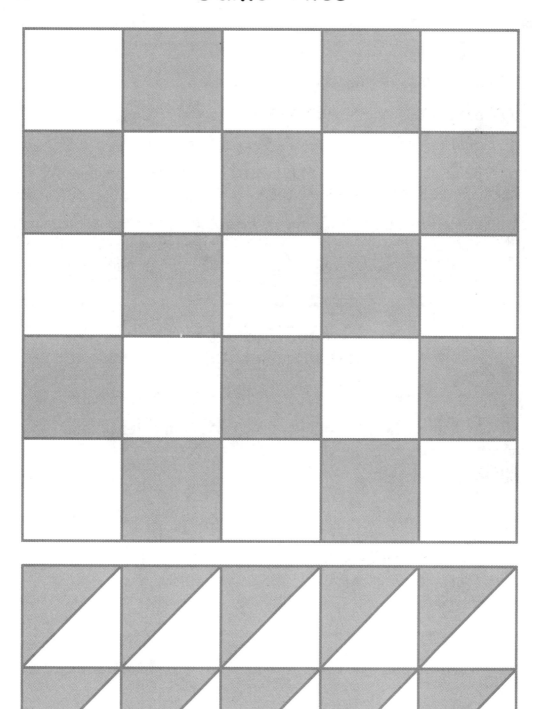

The Skeleton Game

Objectives:

- ❧ To review the bones of the skeleton.
- ❧ To learn questioning strategies.
- ❧ To listen for clues and think of answers.

Materials: a chart of the human skeletal system (see page 57)

The Game: The teacher says, "I'm thinking of a bone of the human body. Use your questioning skills to find out which bone it is."

The Rules: The students may not use the name of the bone. The teacher should have them think of some strategies they could use. The students should talk quietly together and find some strategies to use. Allow the students 12 total questions.

Sample Dialogue

(*S* = student, *T* = teacher)

S: Is it the clavicle?

T: You may not use the name of the bone, but you could point and say, "Is it this one?"

S: Is it in the top half of the body?

T: Show me where the top and bottom half are joined.

S: Here. (*Student shows teacher where the body line is.*)

T: It is in the bottom half.

S: Is it a round, long bone?

T: No.

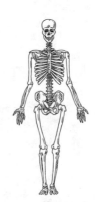

The Skeleton Game *(cont.)*

The Human Skeletal System

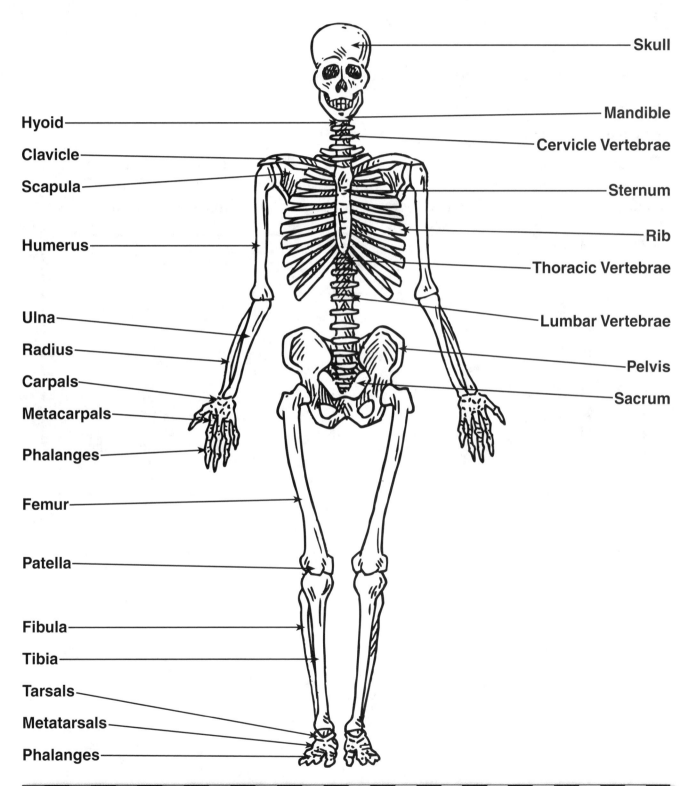

Skull

Mandible

Cervicle Vertebrae

Sternum

Rib

Thoracic Vertebrae

Lumbar Vertebrae

Pelvis

Sacrum

Hyoid

Clavicle

Scapula

Humerus

Ulna

Radius

Carpals

Metacarpals

Phalanges

Femur

Patella

Fibula

Tibia

Tarsals

Metatarsals

Phalanges

The Animals Game

Objectives:

- ❧ To develop thinking strategies.
- ❧ To learn precise questioning techniques.
- ❧ To listen to others' questions.

Materials: animal cards (see pages 59 and 60)

The Game: The teacher selects an animal card. The students have 10 questions as a class to find out the name of the mystery animal. Students may talk to their neighbors about strategies to use. They may not use the name of any animal in their questions.

Sample Dialogue
(*S* = student, *T* = teacher)

S: Does it fly?

T: No.

S: How many legs does it have?

T: Fewer than four.

S: Does it lay eggs?

T: No.

S: Does it live in the water?

T: Yes.

S: Does it start with an F?

T: No, it starts with a letter in the second half of the alphabet.

Variation: Have a student select an animal card and lead the rest of the class through the questioning process.

Bear   Frog   Owl

The Animal Game (cont.)

Animal Cards

Alligator	Bat	Bear
Bee	Butterfly	Cat
Crab	Cow	Dog
Dolphin	Eel	Frog

The Animal Game (cont.)

Animal Cards (cont.)

Fly	Horse	Kangaroo
Lion	Lizard	Owl
Penguin	Seahorse	Snake
Spider	Turtle	Walrus

The Checkerboard Game

Objectives:

- ❖ To work with coordinates.
- ❖ To learn to ask skillful questions.
- ❖ To learn to use answers to others' questions.
- ❖ To develop good elimination strategies.

Materials: a checkerboard (see page 63)

The Game: The teacher points out to the class that the checkerboard has numbers on one side and letters on the other. The teacher then reviews the concept by naming squares (E1, F3, etc.). The teacher chooses a square. The students guess which square by asking questions.

Sample Dialogue

(*S* = student, *T* = teacher)

S: What color is it?

T: It is not black.

S: What row is it in?

T: Let's learn rows and columns. (*Demonstrate rows and columns.*) It is in a row that does not have curly lines when you write it.

S: Is it in a column that is an odd number?

T: No, the number of the column is even.

S: I can't think of any more questions.

T: How about asking this question: "If I divide the chart in half, top to bottom, which side would it be on?"

S: What if I did that?

T: Ask the "if" question to get practice.

The Checkerboard Game (cont.)

Here is a variation on the Checkerboard Game.

Objectives:

- ⚭ To work with coordinates.
- ⚭ To learn to ask more complex questions.
- ⚭ To learn to organize thoughts and think through answers.
- ⚭ To learn reasoning skills.

Materials: a checkerboard (see page 63)

The Game: The teacher shows the checkerboard. The teacher then challenges the student to a harder version of the first checkerboard game. The teacher has the students ask two questions at a time. For example, "Is it black and in row three?" The teacher can give one of three types of answers: one is true, neither is true, or both are true.

Sample Dialogue

(*S* = student, *T* = teacher)

S: Is it black and in row two?

T: Neither is true.

S: It must be white!

T: Good.

S: Is it on the right side of the chart and white?

T: (*The teacher draws an imaginary line to divide the chart into left and right sides*). One of those is true.

S: Is it on the perimeter?

T: What is the second part of the question?

S: And is it black?

T: Neither of those is true.

The Checkerboard Game (cont.)

Checkerboard

The Combination Game

Objectives:

- To review addition facts.
- To work with coordinates.
- To learn question asking.
- To recognize patterns.

Materials: the game chart from page 65

The Game: The teacher presents students with a chart. The teacher then picks a number on the chart. The students may find out what it is by asking questions. They may not use any number greater than 10 in their questions.

Sample Dialogue

(*S* = student, *T* = teacher)

S: What number is it? Can you point it out?

T: Yes, I can, but I want you to find it.

S: Is it an even number?

T: Yes.

S: Is it in the bottom half of the chart?

T: Yes. (*Teacher draws a line to show the bottom.*)

S: Is it on the right half of the chart?

T: Yes (*Teacher draws a line to show the right half.*)

S: Is it a two-digit number?

T: Yes.

S: What do the digits add up to?

T: Seven

	1	2	3	4	5	6	7	8	9	10
1	2	3	4	5	6	7	8	9	10	11
2	3	4	5	6	7	8	9	10	11	12
3	4	5	6	7	8	9	10	11	12	13
4	5	6	7	8	9	10	11	12	13	14
5	6	7	8	9	10	11	12	13	14	15
6	7	8	9	10	11	12	13	14	15	16
7	8	9	10	11	12	13	14	15	16	17
8	9	10	11	12	13	14	15	16	17	18
9	10	11	12	13	14	15	16	17	18	19
10	11	12	13	14	15	16	17	18	19	20

The Combination Game (cont.)

Game Chart

	1	2	3	4	5	6	7	8	9	10
1	2	3	4	5	6	7	8	9	10	11
2	3	4	5	6	7	8	9	10	11	12
3	4	5	6	7	8	9	10	11	12	13
4	5	6	7	8	9	10	11	12	13	14
5	6	7	8	9	10	11	12	13	14	15
6	7	8	9	10	11	12	13	14	15	16
7	8	9	10	11	12	13	14	15	16	17
8	9	10	11	12	13	14	15	16	17	18
9	10	11	12	13	14	15	16	17	18	19
10	11	12	13	14	15	16	17	18	19	20

The Capitals Game

Objectives:

- To review state capitals.
- To review direction.
- To develop question-theory-question strategies.

Materials: a chart listing each state along with its number and year of admission into the United States, population, capital, and most populous city (see pages 67–68); a map of the United States (page 23)

The Game: The students are presented with a list of state facts. Teacher may wish to at first focus on one type of state fact, such as state capitals. In this case, the teacher will say, "I am thinking of a state capital. Use your questioning skills to determine which one I am thinking of." Every time the student asks a question, the teacher will not only give them an answer, but also a clue. Teacher may wish to use such clues as state number, the year the state officially became a state, and the state's population. All of this information is provided on the charts on pages 67 and 68.

Sample Dialogue
(*S* = student, *T* = teacher)

S: Is it Salem?

T: No, but it begins with a letter that is in the second half of the alphabet.

S: Is it Sacramento?

T: No, it is from a state that is east of California.

S: Does the state it's in begin with a letter in the first half of the alphabet?

T: Yes, and here's another clue: the state was admitted into the United States in the 19th century.

List of States

State	Number	Year	Population*	Capital	Most Populous City
Alabama	22	1819	4,557,808	Montgomery	Birmingham
Alaska	49	1959	663,661	Juneau	Anchorage
Arizona	48	1912	5,939,292	Phoenix	Phoenix
Arkansas	25	1836	2,779,154	Little Rock	Little Rock
California	31	1850	36,132,147	Sacramento	Los Angeles
Colorado	38	1876	4,665,177	Denver	Denver
Connecticut	5	1788	3,510,297	Hartford	Bridgeport
Delaware	1	1787	843,524	Dover	Wilmington
Florida	27	1845	17,789,864	Tallahassee	Jacksonville
Georgia	4	1788	9,072,576	Atlanta	Atlanta
Hawaii	50	1959	1,275,194	Honolulu	Honolulu
Idaho	43	1890	1,429,096	Boise	Boise
Illinois	21	1818	12,763,371	Springfield	Chicago
Indiana	19	1816	6,271,973	Indianapolis	Indianapolis
Iowa	29	1846	2,966,334	Des Moines	Des Moines
Kansas	34	1861	2,744,687	Topeka	Wichita
Kentucky	15	1792	4,173,405	Frankfort	Louisville
Louisiana	18	1812	4,523,628	Baton Rouge	New Orleans
Maine	23	1820	1,321,505	Augusta	Portland
Maryland	7	1788	5,600,388	Annapolis	Baltimore
Massachusetts	6	1788	6,398,743	Boston	Boston
Michigan	26	1837	10,120,860	Lansing	Detroit
Minnesota	32	1858	5,132,799	St. Paul	Minneapolis
Mississippi	20	1817	2,921,088	Jackson	Jackson
Missouri	24	1821	5,800,310	Jefferson City	Kansas City

* population figures as of 2005

List of States (cont.)

State	Number	Year	Population*	Capital	Most Populous City
Montana	41	1889	935,670	Helena	Billings
Nebraska	37	1867	1,758,787	Lincoln	Omaha
Nevada	36	1864	2,414,807	Carson City	Las Vegas
New Hampshire	9	1788	1,309,940	Concord	Manchester
New Jersey	3	1787	8,717,925	Trenton	Newark
New Mexico	47	1912	1,928,384	Santa Fe	Albuquerque
New York	11	1788	19,254,630	Albany	New York
North Carolina	12	1789	8,683,242	Raleigh	Charlotte
North Dakota	39	1889	636,677	Bismarck	Fargo
Ohio	17	1803	11,464,042	Columbus	Columbus
Oklahoma	46	1907	3,547,884	Oklahoma City	Oklahoma City
Oregon	33	1859	3,641,056	Salem	Portland
Pennsylvania	2	1787	12,429,616	Harrisburg	Philadelphia
Rhode Island	13	1790	1,076,189	Providence	Providence
South Carolina	8	1788	4,255,083	Columbia	Columbia
South Dakota	40	1889	775,933	Pierre	Sioux Falls
Tennessee	16	1796	5,962,959	Nashville	Memphis
Texas	18	1845	22,859,968	Austin	Houston
Utah	45	1896	2,469,585	Salt Lake City	Salt Lake City
Vermont	14	1791	623,050	Montpelier	Burlington
Virginia	10	1788	7,567,465	Richmond	Virginia Beach
Washington	42	1889	6,287,759	Olympia	Seattle
West Virginia	35	1863	1,816,856	Charleston	Charleston
Wisconsin	30	1848	5,536,201	Madison	Milwaukee
Wyoming	44	1890	509,294	Cheyenne	Cheyenne

* population figures as of 2005

The Directions Game

Objectives:

- ◆ To learn to follow directions.
- ◆ Cement directions in students' minds.
- ◆ Develop question-theory-question cycle.
- ◆ To listen to other students.

Materials: map of the U.S. (see page 23); maps of other countries, continents, etc., may also be used (see pages 70–71 for a world map; use tape or glue to connect these pages at the dotted line)

The Game: The students must find the state (province, country, etc.) that the teacher is thinking of. The students name the state (province, country, etc.), then listens to the teacher's response.

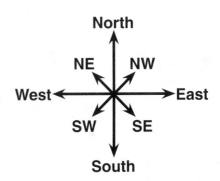

The Rules: This game may work best if students are limited to 15 questions. Have students ask their questions in the form of the complete sentences.

Note: You may wish to go review directions with students prior to playing this game.

Sample Dialogue

(*S* = student, *T* = teacher)

S: Is it Kansas?

T: No. Go north.

S: Is it Michigan?

T: No. Go east.

S: Is it New York?

T: No. Go southwest.

S: Is it Ohio?

T: No. Go west.

Variation: Incorporate information from the Capitals Game (pages 66–68) into this game.

The Directions Game (cont.)

World Map

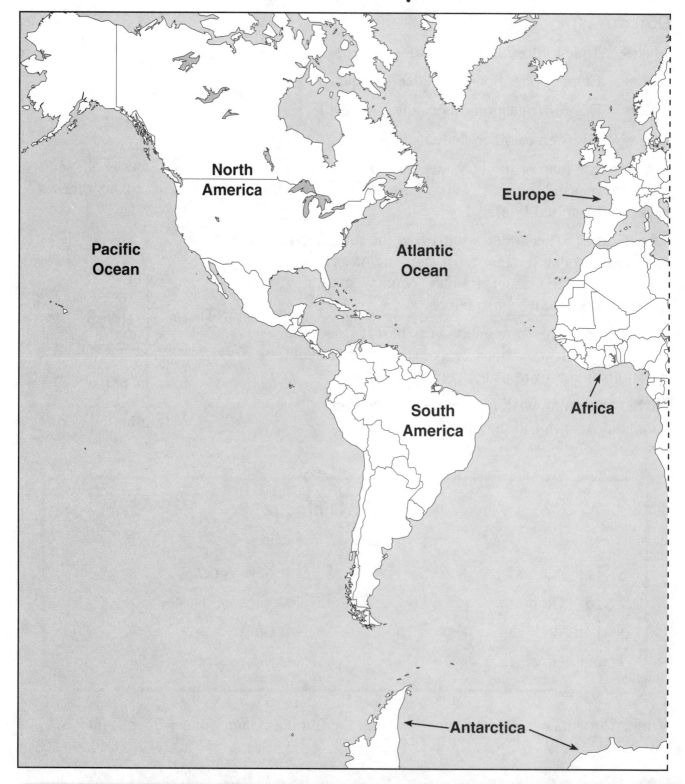

World Map *(cont.)*

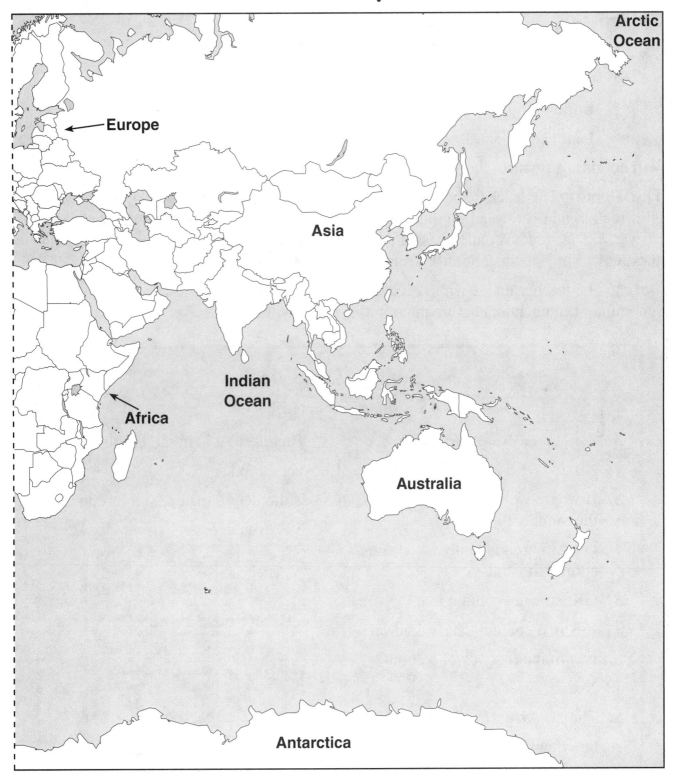

The Fractions Game

Objectives:

- Review fraction terminology.
- Ask precise questions.
- Build on other questions.
- Learn coordinates.

Materials: a fraction chart (see page 73)

The Game: The teacher shows a fraction chart to the class and says, "I am thinking of a fraction that is located on this chart. Use your questioning skills to determine the answer." The students must guess the fraction that the teacher is thinking of by asking questions. Students may not ask a single fraction question.

Note: The teacher may wish to review fractions and related terminology (e.g., denominator, numerator) before playing this game with students.

Sample Dialogue

(*S* = student, *T* = teacher)

S: Is it an underlined fraction?

T: No.

S: How are we supposed to guess the number?

T: One way might be to ask what column it is in.

S: OK, so what column is it?

T: It is in a column that is a vowel.

S: Is it in the first vowel column?

T: No.

S: The last vowel?

T: No, therefore . . .

S: Therefore, it is in the E column?

T: Very good.

S: Is the denominator even or odd?

T: It is even.

	A	B	C	D	E	F	G	H	I
1	1/10	5/25	10/10	5/7	7/8	6/18	6/8	4/8	9/10
2	5/3	3/9	6/6	1/8	11/20	4/6	4/9	7/16	8/10
3	4/8	1/7	3/6	1/9	1/4	2/9	14/8	1/5	3/4
4	1/7	2/10	5/10	6/7	2/8	1/19	2/10	5/8	4/7
5	4/7	6/8	1/4	1/3	11/11	3/6	7/10	17/22	3/6
6	5/6	4/8	5/7	4/8	3/10	1/3	6/5	3/7	1/2
7	8/9	1/9	2/7	9/4	7/10	2/3	3/8	6/10	7/7
8	1/2	2/21	2/4	2/2	5/8	9/8	6/9	3/16	4/7
9	6/5	4/17	5/9	3/14	2/13	7/3	13/8	4/13	5/11
10	6/11	2/16	9/11	14/11	5/2	3/19	9/9	8/7	4/23
11	16/14	7/8	3/10	5/5	16/16	19/12	7/6	1/12	11/6
12	4/10	6/9	14/8	15/7	3/2	5/3	11/12	9/19	4/3

The Fractions Game (cont.)

Fractions Chart

	A	B	C	D	E	F	G	H	I
1	1/10	5/25	10/10	5/7	7/8	6/18	6/8	4/8	9/10
2	5/3	3/9	6/6	1/8	11/20	4/6	4/9	7/16	8/10
3	4/8	1/7	3/6	1/9	1/4	2/9	14/8	1/5	3/4
4	1/7	2/10	5/10	6/7	2/8	1/19	2/10	5/8	4/7
5	4/7	6/8	1/4	1/3	11/11	3/6	7/10	17/22	3/6
6	5/6	4/8	5/7	4/8	3/10	1/3	6/5	3/7	1/2
7	8/9	1/9	2/7	9/4	7/10	2/3	3/8	6/10	7/7
8	1/2	2/21	2/4	2/2	5/8	9/8	6/9	3/16	4/7
9	6/5	4/17	5/9	3/14	2/13	7/3	13/8	4/13	5/11
10	6/11	2/16	9/11	14/11	5/2	3/19	9/9	8/7	4/23
11	16/14	7/8	3/10	5/5	16/16	19/12	7/6	1/12	11/6
12	4/10	6/9	14/8	15/7	3/2	5/3	11/12	9/19	4/3

The Fractions Game (cont.)

Here is a variation of the Fractions Game.

Objective:

- ❧ Review fraction concepts and terminology.
- ❧ Explore mental math.
- ❧ Refine questioning strategies.
- ❧ Develop the data-theory cycle.

Materials: 20 cards cut from red construction paper (each card should have a number from 1–20 written on it); 20 cards cut from blue construction paper (each card should have a number from 1–20 written on it)

The Game: The teacher presents the class with two sets of cards. The red cards represent numerators, and the blue cards represent denominators. The teacher may wish to allow students to practice making fractions with the cards to get the idea. Students must then arrange the cards to guess the number that the teacher is thinking of while asking questions.

Sample Dialogue

(*S* = student, *T* = teacher)

S: Is the top number bigger than the bottom?

T: No.

S: Is the fraction bigger than one-half?

T: No.

S: Is the fraction one-half?

T: No, but it is equivalent to one-half?

S: Do either of the top and bottom numbers have two digits?

T: No.

3 10 17

The Math Facts Game

Objectives:

- ❧ Explore mental math.
- ❧ Review addition, subtraction, multiplication, and division concepts.
- ❧ Refine questioning strategies.
- ❧ Develop thinking strategies.
- ❧ Work in a team.

The Game: The teacher says, "I am thinking of an addition problem. One of the numbers in the equation is 12. Ask questions to figure out the entire equation."

Sample Dialogue
(*S* = student, *T* = teacher)

S: Is 12 the answer to the equation?

T: Yes.

S: Are the other two number single-digit numbers?

T: Yes.

S: Is one of the numbers 6?

T: You can't ask that question. Try a different approach.

S: Are both of the numbers even?

T: No.

Variation: Use this same line of questioning for subtraction, multiplication, and division equations. Have students guess the operation, as well as the numbers involved in the equation.

Note: For this game, you may wish to use the red and blue cards created for the Fractions Game (see page 74). You may wish to create a third set of cards that has the operation signs (+, −, x, ÷) on them.

The 1–100 Game

Objective:

- ↞ To find number patterns.
- ↞ To learn some prime numbers.
- ↞ To learn new thinking strategies.
- ↞ To learn exact questions.

Materials: a chart of the numbers 1 through 100 (see page 77)

The Game: The teacher shows a number chart. On this chart, the prime numbers are shown in italic (slanted) type. The teacher then thinks of a number on the chart. The students must guess the number by asking questions. The students may not guess any single number (for example, "Is it 26?").

Sample Dialogue

(*S* = student, *T* = teacher)

S: What column is it in?

T: It is in an even-numbered column.

S: Is it in the fifties row?

T: No. You might want to ask a question that will give you more information. A better question might be, "Is it above the fifties row?"

S: Is it above the fifties row?

T: No.

S: Is it underlined?

T: Yes, it is.

S: If I divide the chart on the "E" column, is it on the left side?

T: No.

S: Why are some numbers underlined, and others are not?

T: See if you can figure out what's different about the numbers.

S: The underlined numbers are odd.

T: But not all of the odd numbers are underlined. And look at the "2."

The 1–100 Game (cont.)

Number Chart

A	B	C	D	E	F	G	H	I	J
1	2	3	4	5	6	7	8	9	10
11	12	13	14	15	16	17	18	19	20
21	22	23	24	25	26	27	28	29	30
31	32	33	34	35	36	37	38	39	40
41	42	43	44	45	46	47	48	49	50
51	52	53	54	55	56	57	58	59	60
61	62	63	64	65	66	67	68	69	70
71	72	73	74	75	76	77	78	79	80
81	82	83	84	85	86	87	88	89	90
91	92	93	94	95	96	97	98	99	100

The Triangle Game

Objectives:

- Review finding patterns.
- Explore mental math.
- Refine questioning strategies.
- Further develop the thinking strategies (data-theory-data).

Materials: a copy of Pascal's Triangle (see page 79)

The Game: The teacher shows Pascal's Triangle and discusses some patterns in the triangle (horizontal, diagonal, above addition, etc.). The teacher chooses a number from the triangle. The students must guess the number without naming it.

Note: Pascal's Triangle was originally developed in Ancient China, but it is named for Blaise Pascal, a 17th-century French mathematician who described many of its patterns. Each number in the triangle is found by adding the two numbers directly above it. (If there is no number above it to either side, add zero.) Many mathematical patterns are formed by the triangle. Detailed information on Pascal's Triangle is readily available on the Internet. Just type "Pascal's Triangle" into any search engine for a list of websites.

Sample Dialogue

(*S* = student, *T* = teacher)

S: What row is it in?

T: OK, I'll number the rows. (*The teacher numbers the rows.*) It is in an even-numbered row.

S: Is it a one- or two-digit number?

T: The number has two digits.

S: Is it 20?

T: You can't ask that.

S: Does the number repeat itself across the row?

T: Yes, it does.

S: Is the number even or odd?

T: The number is odd.

The Triangle Game *(cont.)*

Pascal's Triangle

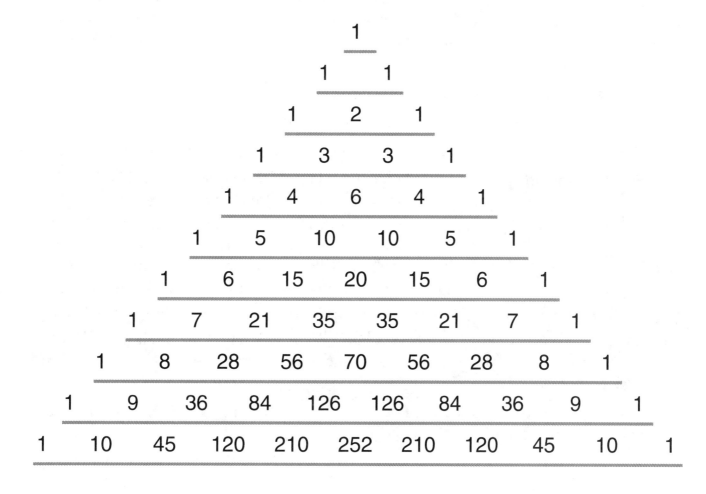

Inquiry Problems

Inquiry problems require longer periods of time or can be played in installments. Some games could go on for months. Inquiry problems give students one element from an unusual event and ask them to fill in the rest of the elements. The events can be taken from real newspaper stories. Inquiry problems are at the heart of the questioning games found in this book.

Objective:

- To learn to ask questions in a classroom setting.

- To learn how to ask different types of questions.

- To learn the data-theory cycle (data produces a theory, a theory is checked to produce more data, the process is not done until the answer is reached).

- To examine cause-and-effect relationships.

- To learn that answers lead to more questions.

- To experience achieving the answer with one's own thinking process.

The Game: The teacher says, "I'm going to describe something that has happened and your challenge is to find out why it happened." These problems take a fair amount of skill on the teacher's part to turn them into a true inquiry through question asking. Two things need to be observed:

1. When students ask, "Is it because of . . . ," they are asking you to verify if they are right. It is their job to determine the answer.

2. When they ask, "Does it have anything to do with . . . ?" they are asking the same thing.

At these points in the process, you have to gently remind them that you are not there to think for them but rather to provide information. In the beginning, some students might get frustrated with the new approach by the teacher. They want direct answers, not the indirect answers given by the teacher. One has to really understand the process and teach students how to arrive at the answers themselves.

Note: Any appropriate newspaper story will work well for these problems. Events that have an effect brought on by unusual causes will keep the students intrigued and asking questions. The following resource is an excellent source of unusual (but real) newspaper articles: Fineman, Susan R. *Read All About It! (Grades 6–7).* Teacher Created Resources, 2006.